If You Were Me and Lived in... Viking Europe

By Carole P. Roman

Illustrated by Mateya Arkova

For David

Copyright 2015 Carole P. Roman All rights reserved.
ISNB-10: 1-947118-15-3 ISBN-13: 978-1-947118-15-7
Library of Congress Control Number: 2012921018
CreateSpace Independent Publishing Platform,
North Charleston, SC

If you were me and lived during Viking times, you would be born sometime in the year 870 AD in the northern part of Europe over eleven hundred and forty years ago. Your home could have been on the coast of Norway.

This is what a town in Norway looks like now.

This is what the landscape might have looked like in your village hundreds of years ago.

Some say the word Viking (Vyk-ing) is from the Norse word vik (vyk), which meant bay or creek. Others say it meant overseas expedition. Either way, people associated it with those who came from the North.

A Viking was an individual who went on those expeditions. Some of these explorers were known to travel plundering foreign towns, taking both prisoners and belongings. However, Vikings were also brave explorers, settlers, and experienced traders.

By the time you were born in the year 870 AD, many had traded their swords for farming tools and created towns to open up trade with new populations.

When a person traveled on his ship for trade or war, he was known as a Viking. When they stayed at home and tended their farms, historians considered them Scandinavians (Skan-duh-ney-vee-ans). When they moved and settled in foreign lands, they were called Norsemen (Nor-se-men).

Your name might have been Knut (Kah-noot) or Ulf (Ul-uff) if you were a boy and Sigrid (Seeg-freed) or Hilde (Hill-da) if you were a girl.

Each name meant something: Knut meant knot, Ulf was the word for wolf, Sigrid was a beautiful woman, and Hilde meant fight. Why do you think they named a son knot and a daughter fight?

Most people went by two names: their given name and their family name. They were usually called after their father, so if Knut's dad was named Eric, he was known as Knut Ericson (Er-ik-son). His daughter would be called Hilde Ericdottir (Er-ik-dot-tar).

Vikings were hearty seafaring people who liked to explore and find places to trade. They were known to travel to other countries, colonizing outposts and creating settlements in far-reaching lands.

Some were more militaristic than others and took over towns by force, changing the way people lived. Others wanted to exchange products from their land and bring home new merchandise.

Vikings were famous for traveling far from home. Some, like your uncle, went to Normandy in Europe where the Franks lived and found a settlement there. Others, like your father, loved to travel to exotic ports and bring home new products. He was a prosperous merchant who had sailed as far as the Baltic Sea to bring back interesting items like amber for jewelry, salt, wine, and glass.

The only coins minted in Scandinavia (Skan-duh-ney-vee-uh) were pennies. Some believe that the penny, like the Scandinavian word for money, got its name from the pans that were melted into coins. In the old Danish language, a small pan was called a penninge (pen-ne-gee) and could be the root of the word.

If you were born to a Viking family, you would be in one of three classes.

If your parents were wealthy, you might be a Jarl (Yaerl). They had many horses, a fine, long house, and owned slaves. Jarls ran the government and were influential people in the society.

Karls (Carl-s) were free peasants or farmers. They owned farms, land, and cattle. Their lives were filled with the hard work of plowing fields, running farms, and milking the cows.

The last segment of society were the thralls. Thralls (Throls) were often captured in raids and brought back to be slaves.

They did all the hard labor from working on the farms to building forts in your village. If they had children, they too were a thrall. They were treated terribly and not well liked.

Your home would be shaped similar to a ship with oval sides. You lived in the house with thirty other people, including the thralls your father brought back from his trading expeditions. Family was important, so many of your aunts, uncles, and cousins on both your mother and father's side made their home with you.

Your father had to help any family member in trouble, and they, in turn, owed their allegiance to your family. The sense of obligation extended as far as your fourth cousin. They all knew you could depend on them, and they could rely on you.

A portion of the big room was walled off for the animals, but you could hear them stamping their feet and making noises all night long.

Sturdy oak poles held the sides of your home, and there was a thick thatched roof that kept the rain out. The floor was stamped earth, strewn with straw to keep it warm. There were no windows; the only light came from lamps made from soapstone or iron. These lamps were simple open bowls that were suspended from metal poles stuck in the ground.

The inside of your house consisted of a wide area with a firepit in the center to both heat the room and cook your meals. Long benches covered in animal fur flanked the center, and that is where everybody slept at night. There was a walled off room in the back where your parents slept in a bed closet. On the other side was a storeroom for all your supplies. Next to it was another room called the dairy with three large vats for storing the milk from the cows with a smithy to make metal objects like horseshoes and tools. In the rear was a special room with a row of benches and a long trench to be used as a latrine (la-treen). This kept human waste away from your water supply.

Your grandfather spent many hours carving useful things for your home. He taught you to find thick wood to create fanciful designs.

His expertise was valuable when they built your father's ship. Your father had two ships. The first one was a knarr (knorr). It was sixty feet long with a tall mast. Its hull was rounder than the other ships in your village, and it went on long voyages, bringing back exciting products in its deep holds.

Your father had a crew of forty sailors, and you couldn't wait for the day you would be old enough to join him on an adventure. The other ship was a byrding (bird-ing) that was used for short trips to trade the many things brought back from long distance journeys.

Of course, it didn't compare to the longboat with their colorful, billowing sails that traveled on the high seas. The multi-oared ships were used to raid the coastal towns of Europe.

Your mother was in charge of the inside household while your father handled most of the work outside when he wasn't traveling. She prepared all the food, did the laundry, used the spinning wheel to make thread, and worked the loom to create cloth. She also made cheese and preserved meats and vegetables for the long winter months when there was nothing fresh to eat.

Food was plentiful. You were used to eating lots of seafood. This year, your father included you when they hunted whales, walruses, and seals. You loved the rich meat and fought over the seal's flipper with your younger brother. Herring, cod, mussels, and shrimp were always on the table.

Horse meat and mutton were special treats. Your mother tended the hens with your many sisters, but you and your brother hunted the wild ducks that thrived near the water. Catching ducks was important because not only was the meat welcomed at the table, but also your mother used the feathers and down for insulation in clothes and blankets to keep you warm.

Your father had a herd of sheep that he used for a food source, yarn, and trading.

Of course, your mother was known for her ale made with barley grown on the family farm. She also made bjórr (bor), a fruity wine. You were not allowed to drink the wine your father imported from the south. That was reserved for his friends when they visited. On special occasions, your mother would make mead, which was ale sweetened with honey. Your father would bring home elk or reindeer for the feast days.

Guests drank from animal horns that were pointed on the bottom so they could never put them down. This meant they had to drink up at once or pass their vessel around.

You and the other children were given wooden cups to drink from so you could finish your ale more slowly than the others.

Your diet was filled with fruit, nuts, cheeses, sausage, porridge, bread, and berries.

Your sister had to collect the hazelnuts from where they fell from the trees. They were used in cooking or eating as a snack.

The walnuts gathered were used to dye clothing. Nothing was wasted! Your mother had a large garden filled with turnips, spinach, cabbages, leeks, peas, and onions too.

Moder (Mo-der), which is what you called your mother, cooked everything in a large cauldron or cooking pot in your home. Sometimes she heated stones and threw them into the water to make the liquid hotter. She also grilled meat on a spit or buried it in a bed of hot stones to roast. She would prepare meat by pickling, smoking, drying, and salting it to keep for the long winter months.

Your mother needed a lot of salt for cooking. You and your brother brought buckets of seawater home. She boiled the seawater in a large pot until it evaporated, leaving a large supply of salt.

Your mother seasoned food with homegrown spices like caraway, mustard, dill, coriander, and horseradish. Since your father was rather wealthy, she had a box of black pepper from across the sea.

You ate your meals using a short bladed knife or your fingers taking the food from flat wooden bowls. You had a spoon carved from a deer's antler for the messy meals. You never wanted to waste a drop of Moder's tasty stews.

Your brothers, sisters and you dressed similarly to your parents. In the summer, your wore lightweight linen trousers under a long linen tunic called a kyrtill (kur-till). It was cinched at your waist with a leather belt. You were given an elaborate buckle for your birthday and proud of it.

You pulled your shirt over your head and made sure that none of your chest showed because that was considered to look feminine. The sleeves were long and dangled past your wrists. You were wealthy, so you wore this colored shirt over a light linen undertunic. You always made sure everyone could see you wore two shirts, so they would know you came from a privileged home.

Every household had a loom and spinning wheel. Your mother and sisters made all your clothes by spinning the wool and weaving cloth. Moder taught your sisters how to use a loom to make cloth. They used flax fibers for linen and sheep wool for winter material.

For the winter, your clothing was made from wool. Your shoes were made from leather. You wore thick leggings to keep your legs warm. You had a long woolen cloak and a beautifully carved bone to fasten it. Your father had a mantle, which was a much fancier cloak, trimmed with fur with a heavy pin filled with precious stones worn on his shoulder. He always made sure that his right arm remained uncovered, so he could retrieve his sword if he needed it. Your mother spent hours embroidering beautiful designs on the back of the cloak. The more colorful his clothing, the wealthier he was. This proclaimed to your village that he was as successful as he was important.

In the deep winter, your mother made you a höttr (hou-ter) or a hood that covered both your head and shoulders. Other times, you wore a plain cap or hat. You were taught that it was illegal to pull a hat off someone's head. If the hat had a chin strap and was pulled backward, the punishment could be banishment or even worse.

Since you had no pockets in your clothing, you used a leather pouch to hold what you needed to carry around with you.

Your sisters wore woolen dresses called hangerocks (hang-er-ocks) that fell to their shins over an ankle-length linen shift. Their necklines were fastened with beautiful brooches, and shoulder straps held their overdresses in place. These pins were called turtle brooches because they looked like the shells of a turtle.

The older girls had necklaces suspended between the pins of colorful glass beads and shells your father brought back from his travels. Your mother wore a wimple (wim-pil), which is a close fitting scarf that kept her blonde hair hidden. She wore her scissors, knife, and other useful objects around her neck for easy access. You carved a needle case from an animal's bone for her to store her sewing needles.

Your mother wore a lot of jewelry. She had brooches, pins, necklaces, and rings that your father brought back from all over the world. Most of it was silver; there was some gold, and many had stones like amber and lapis in them.

The winters were harsh and could be deadly if you weren't prepared.

Your mother always kept spare clothing on hand for any traveler who may need it and got stuck or lost in the cold, wet weather. You always made people feel welcomed if they traveled through and needed help. You were taught that someday it might be you who needs some food or warmth when you were out in the world.

An entire year consisted of a time of light (summer) and a time of darkness (winter). Summer lasted from April to October, so that meant winter was October to April. You measured your age by the number of winters you lived through.

Summer was for making and preparing; winter was a time of using what you prepared.

The day was divided into time of light and time of darkness. You measured your day by the meals you ate: dagmal (dag-mal) was your day-meal at nine in the morning and nattmal (nat-mal) for your night-meal was usually at nine in the evening.

Your whole family was well-groomed. Your father wore many necklaces, pins called brooches, and a thick belt buckle made from gold and silver. He had eight arm rings on each of his muscled arms. When the sun shone on them, it looked like he was made of metal. These bracelets were important. The king gave them to your father for his service to the crown.

The Vikings did not have an army, and when they were threatened, the king called all his powerful men to bring troops. Your father brought many men to defend the village. As an honor for doing this, the king presented him with many arm rings for being a helpful general or stallari (sta-lar-ree).

There was an old saga (sa-ga) or poem written in Norse about your father's bravery. That had happened many years before you were born, but you would love to have a story told about your strength and courage too.

You spent your days learning how to survive, including skills of shooting with a bow and arrow, preparing your catch for dinner, or watching other adults work. You were expected to learn from everyone in your village, whether it was making furniture, building a house, or riding a horse. You wished you owned a falcon like the king's son. He tamed the wild bird and used it to hunt ducks and seabirds instead of a bow and arrow.

If you were caught fighting, your parents never punished you. You were expected to learn how to protect and defend yourself.

Soon, you were to be fostered out to another family, and their son was supposed to live in your home. This was done to make special friendships called alliances with other families, so they would help your clan if there was a problem and you would help theirs. You were sad to leave your home, but you knew you would be learning valuable things in your father's ally's house.

Your sisters spent the day learning how to weave, spin wool, sew, cook, and tend the garden. There were no schools like the ones you heard of in southern Europe. They were run by priests from the Roman church.

By the time your sisters were twelve, your father was looking for a suitable husband for them. They were usually married when they reached their fifteenth birthday. Their marriage was crucial to your family. Your father tried to match them with a family that would be an alliance that brought protection and help. Your sister had little to say who her husband was going to be.

Your sister would bring a dowry (dow-ree) of linen, a spinning wheel, loom, and bed into the marriage. Her new husband brought farm animals and some gold and silver jewelry. Eventually, her children would inherit all this property.

Although she was married, she was still considered part of your family, not her husband's. If her spouse turned out to be a bad provider or he mistreated or insulted her family, she could divorce him. It was considered a grave dishonor for a husband to abuse his wife. All she had to do was ask a witness to come into her home and stand near her bed. Once she declared herself finished with him, the marriage was over.

A woman could never be a chief or vote in the assemblies. Women were, however, respected and had more freedom than most of the women in Europe. They managed their household finances and stepped in to make marriages for their children if their husbands weren't there.

You had many activities to do for fun. You were encouraged to throw spears, shoot a bow and arrow, or throw stones as far as you could. You played a game of skill on your father's ship where you stepped from oar to oar on the outside of it, while it was being rowed. This was the hardest thing you tried to do.

You learned to fist fight and juggle with knives, as well as ski and skate. Popular things to do were horse racing and a game called knattleikr (nat-lik-er), which you played on a team using a ball and a bat on the frozen lake. You wore sand and tar on the soles of your shoes so you wouldn't slip.

There was a board game called skaktafl (skat-taf-el) which was a game of war. You used dice carved from stone.

Your sisters loved to dance. You liked to bang on the dishes and tables to make music, but they preferred the fiddles, lyres (ly-er), and lutes that some of your relatives played.

Your mother made feasts that were famous with delicious food and a lot to drink. Afterward, there were verbal duels where guests would take turns insulting each other. Sometimes someone would brag about the things he could do; other times, he would use his wit to make fun of someone else.

Either way, it was done to prove the person wasn't affected by the ale he drank. Your father would close the night by telling sagas or reciting beautiful poems that brought tears to your mother's eyes.

It was often said that your people didn't know how to read and write. This was not true.

You had a special alphabet called runic (roon-ik). There were twenty-four characters. Each character had a name, and each rune (roon) represented not only its sound but also the item for which it was named.

Since rune stones with writing were located in public places, beside the roads, and on bridges, it proved that most everybody could read somewhat.

Your grandmother was a vital person in your village; she was an inciter (in-cy-ter). She had a loud voice, and when she was irritated about something or felt that the community was insulted, she would nag and harangue (har-rang) the men into action. She worried about the town's honor and was known to use her magic to keep them safe.

She was famous for the potions and spells she used to help people. She was brave and smart, and the whole village respected her.

You were taught to worship many gods. There were gods for all the critical aspects of life.

Your family believed in many gods. There were so many gods it was hard to keep track of them. These gods control everything from the stars to the weather. You worried all the time about what things they might do. They could make it storm or have a volcano erupt. They fought among themselves all the time. You wanted to be on their good side and brought them lots of gifts.

You knew they stayed young and powerful by eating magic apples. You made sure to eat lots of apples too.

Your favorite was Thor (Th-or) because he was the god of thunder, but you enjoyed Loki's (Low-kee's) antics too.

So you see, if you were me, how life in Viking times could really be.

Here is a list of some Norse Gods:

Freya (Fre-yah)- the goddess of love and beauty.

Frigg (Frigg)- the goddess of love and marriage. She was able to foresee the future.

Idun (Yuh-done)- the goddess of eternal youth.

Loki (Low-kee)- the god of fire. He was a trouble-maker.

Odin (Oh-din)- the god of war, father to many of the other gods.

Thor (Th-or)- using his hammer to make thunder, he was known for keeping law and order.

Some Important Vikings in History:

Erik the Red (Eric the Red) (950 AD-c.1003 AD)- a famous Norse explorer who founded Greenland. He was called Eric the Red because of his red hair.

Leif Erikson (Leaf Eric-son) (c.970 AD-c.1020 AD)- considered to be the first European to explore North America around the year 1000. He went there about 500 years before Christopher Columbus.

Rollo (Rol-lo) (c.846 AD-c.932 AD)- the first ruler of Normandy, a region in France. He came from a noble warrior Viking family. He had a reputation of being a great leader. He raided the coasts of both Ireland and France.

The king of the area gave him lands to settle if he promised to stop raiding along the river and provide protection from other Vikings. His descendant, William the Conqueror, invaded England in 1066.

Cnut the Great (Ka-nut the Great) (c.995 AD-1035 AD)- the king of Denmark, Norway, England, and parts of Sweden. He was known as a good king.

Swen Forkbeard (S-when Fork-beard) (960 AD-1014 AD)- Cnut the Great's father and king of Denmark, England, and parts of Norway. In the mid-980s, he seized the throne from his father. He was the first Danish King of England.

Sigrid the Haughty (See-grid the Haw-tee) (967 AD-1014 AD)- an important queen who had many sagas written about her generations after she lived.

She was married to Swen Forkbeard of Denmark. Some say she wasn't a real person but described in stories as a combination of many queens.

Unn the Deep Minded (Un-n the Deep Mind-ed) (834 AD-900 AD)- a great leader who sailed her ships and made successful settlements in Iceland.

She freed all her slaves and was regarded as a good leader. She married her children to powerful leaders, making them connected to each other.

Emma of Normandy (Em-ma of Nor-man-de) (c.985 AD-1052 AD)- a medieval queen to two kings, Ethelred the Unready (1002-1016) and Cnut the Great (1017-1035). After both her husbands died, she remained active in politics.

Glossary

ale (aye-I)- a type of beer with a fruity taste.

allegiance (uh-lee-jent-s)- the loyalty to another person or group.

amber (am-burr)- a fossil-like tree resin with a yellowish-brown color. Amber is often used in jewelry.

Baltic Sea (Bal-tic)- an inland sea between Scandinavia and mainland Europe.

banishment (ban-ish-ment)- to be forced to leave a country for good by an authoritative leader as an act of punishment.

barley (bar-lee)- a cereal grain, part of the grass family. Barley is commonly used in soups, stews, and distilled drinks.

bjórr (bor)- a strong alcoholic beverage made with fruit and honey.

byrding (bird-ing)- a boat that carried lightweight freight for merchants.

brooches (bro-chezes)- decorative jewelry worn pinned to clothing.

cauldron (cal-dron)- a large hanging cooking pot.

caraway (car-a-way)- the aromatic seeds used in cooking and for seasoning.

cloak (klok)- outer garment without sleeves worn over clothing.

colonizing (col-uh-nigh-zing)- the settlers who claim land in foreign places and set up homes there.

coriander (co-ree-and-er)- the aromatic seeds used in cooking and for seasoning.

dagmal (dag-mal)- morning meal or breakfast, usually eaten at 9 A.M.

deep-minded (deep-mind-ed)- a thoughtful person.

dill (dil)- the leaves that come from a plant in the celery family. These leaves are used to cook with as a spice either fresh from the plant or dried out.

dowry (dow-ry)- money supplied by a bride's family to her husband upon marriage.

duel (doo-uhl)- a battle royal between two people or parties using deadly weapons.

Ericdottir (Er-ik-dot-tar)- a daughter's last name. Her father's name was Eric, and she was his daughter.

Ericson (Er-ik-son)- a son's last name. His father's name was Eric, and he was Eric's son.

expedition (ex-pe-dit-shun)- a group of people who travel together to a distant place.

exotic (ig-zod-ik)- foreign, different.

falcon (fawl-kun)- a fast-flying bird that can be trained to hunt by swooping and diving to catch its prey.

flax (flaks)- the seeds that hold lots of fiber. The fiber from the seed is used for cloth to make sheets and clothing.

fiddle (fid-del)- violin.

foresee (for-see)- able to see the future.

fostered (faw-stered)- to help nurture, provide, and developmentally grow a child.

Franks (Franks)- an ethnic group who took control of Normandy after the fall of Rome in the 5th century.

hangerocks (hang-er-ocks)- a dress with a wide bottom usually worn over another dress by women during the Viking period.

harangue (har-rang)- nag or lecture.

Hilde (Hill-da)- a popular girl's name in Viking times that means fight.

horseradish (horse-rad-ish)- a plant from the mustard family whose roots are often grounded up and combined with vinegar to made into a condiment.

höttr (hou-ter)- a hood that covers the head and shoulders.

inciter (in-cy-ter)- a person who nags and winds up a crowd to react.

jarls (yaerl)- a Scandinavian noble in ranking right under the king.

karls (carl-s)- the free peasants within the Scandinavian class system.

knarr (nor)- the ships built and used by Vikings for long voyages, sailing the Atlantic Ocean.

knattleikr (nat-lik-er)- an aged ball game played by the Vikings.

Knut (Kah-noot)- a popular boy's name in Viking times that meant knot.

kyrtill (kur-till)- an exterior shirt made of wool and designed to go over a man's top.

lapis (lap-is)- a blue gemstone.

latrine (la-treen)- a toilet.

linen (lin-en)- a fabric made out of flax yarn used to create bedding, clothes, tablecloths, and more.

longboats (long-boats)- the long and narrow Viking ships with one square sail, rowed by eight to ten crewmen.

loom (lum)- a frame or machine for interlacing at right angles two or more sets of threads or yarns to form a cloth.

lute (loot)- stringed instrument.

lyre (ly-er)- a stringed instrument like a harp.

mantle (man-tl)- a men's cloak that is worn over the shoulders.

mead (medd)- an ale-like drink flavored with honey.

militaristic (mil-e-ter-is-tik)- having war-like intent with military operations.

Moder (Mo-der)- Mom

mutton (mut-ton)- the meat of domestic sheep.

mustard (mus-terd)- the crushed seeds of plants that create a yellow paste for seasoning and taste.

nattmal (nat-mal)- the nighttime meal or supper, usually eaten at 9 P.M.

Normandy (Nor-man-de)- a region on the coast of France. The name Normandy originated from the Normans also known as the Northmen who settled in the region.

Norse (nors)- another term for the Northmen in the Scandinavian countries.

Norsemen (Nors-men)- means "men from the north," referred to people from Scandinavia.

Norway (Nor-way)- also known as the Kingdom of Norway. Norway is a northern European country, west of Scandinavia, bordering the Atlantic and Arctic Oceans. The country is famous for its fishing, oil, and wood.

obligation (ob-li-gey-shun)- a commitment made by a person who is morally or lawfully constrained.

penninge (pen-ne-gee)- the Scandinavian word for a copper pan. The word penny is derived from the word penninge.

plundering (pluhn-der-ing)- to steal goods from others by using force and invasion.

porridge (por-ridge)- is a dish made by boiling ground, crushed, or chopped grains in water or milk and served hot in a bowl.

potions (po-shuns)- mixtures believed to magic capabilities.

rune (roon)- any of the characters in an alphabet used by the Northern Europeans, especially Scandinavians, in the Medieval Times.

runic (roo-nik)- an alphabet mostly used by Northern Europeans.

saga (sa-ga)- a long story often in poem form about a great deed or bravery in battle.

Scandinavia (Skan-dun-a-via)- a large peninsula in northwestern Europe, occupied by Norway and Sweden.

Scandinavians (Skan-duh-ney-vee-ans)- the people who stayed at home and farmed the land.

settlements (set-tel-ments)- groups of people who came to an area to settle and farm the land.

shift (shift)- a simple kind of undergarment like a slip.

skaktafl (skat-taf-el)- a board game related to chess.

Sigfrid (Seeg-frred)- a popular girl's name in Viking times that meant a beautiful woman.

smithy (smith-ee)- a blacksmith's workshop.

soapstone (soap-stone)- a talc metamorphic rock with a soap-like feel to the touch.

stallari (sta-lar-ree)- a military general.

thatched (thach-ed)- bundled straw used for a roof.

thralls (throls)- a slave, servant, or captive.

tunic (too-nick)- a loose piece of clothing usually without sleeves that reaches to the knees and worn by men and women.

Ulf (Ul-uff)- a popular boy's name in Viking times. The name means wolf.

undertunic (under-too-nik)- a shirt worn under another shirt.

vik (vyk)- a bay or inlet in Norse.

Viking (Vyk-ing)- Scandinavian pirates who raided and settled in parts of northwestern Europe in the 8th–11th centuries.

wimple (wim-pil)- a cloth headdress worn by women that covers the head, neck, and sides of the face.

www.ingramcontent.com/pod-product-compliance
Lightning Source LLC
Chambersburg PA
CBHW050756110526
44588CB00002B/13